VIET NAM

TRACE TAYLOR

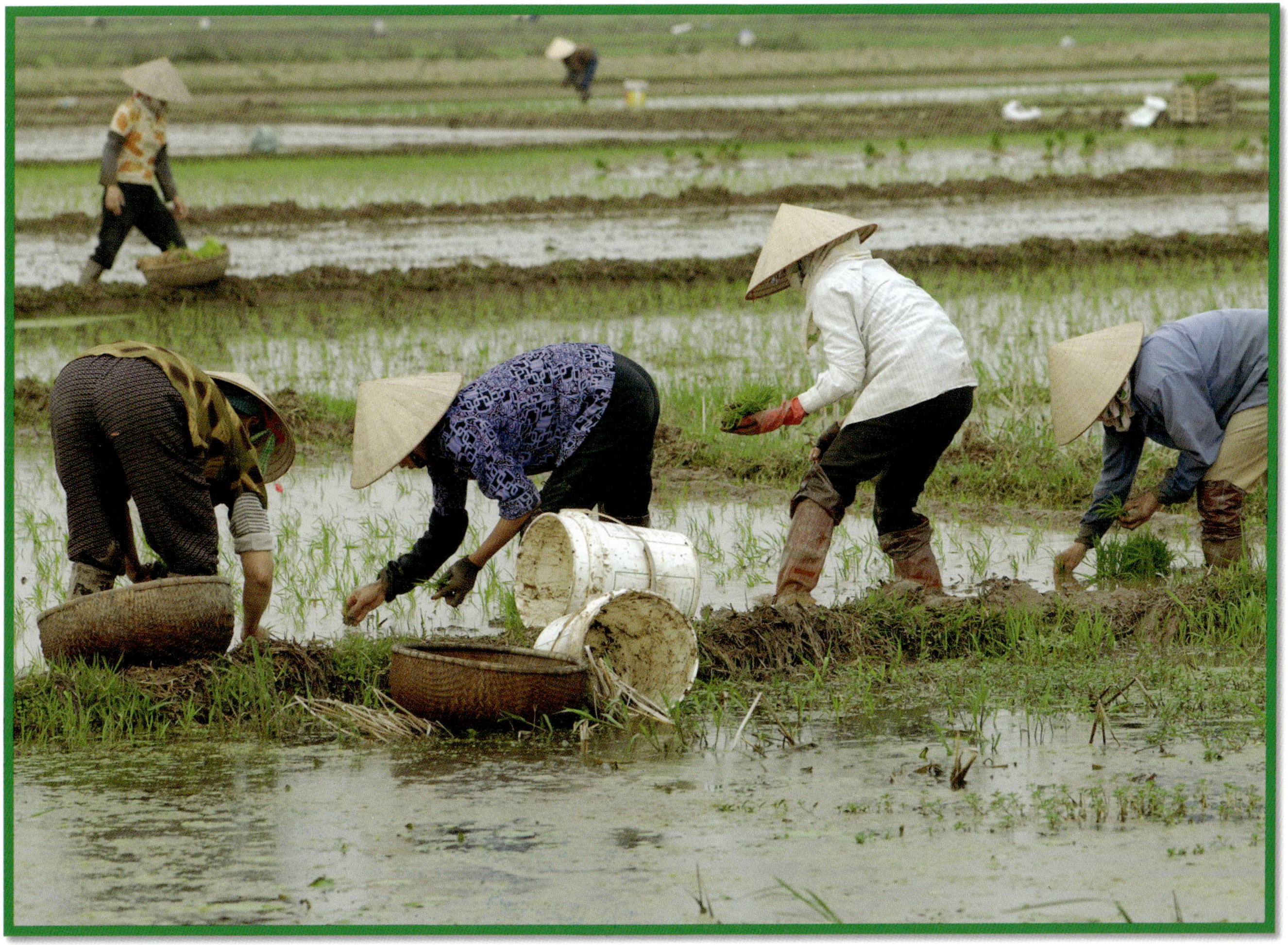

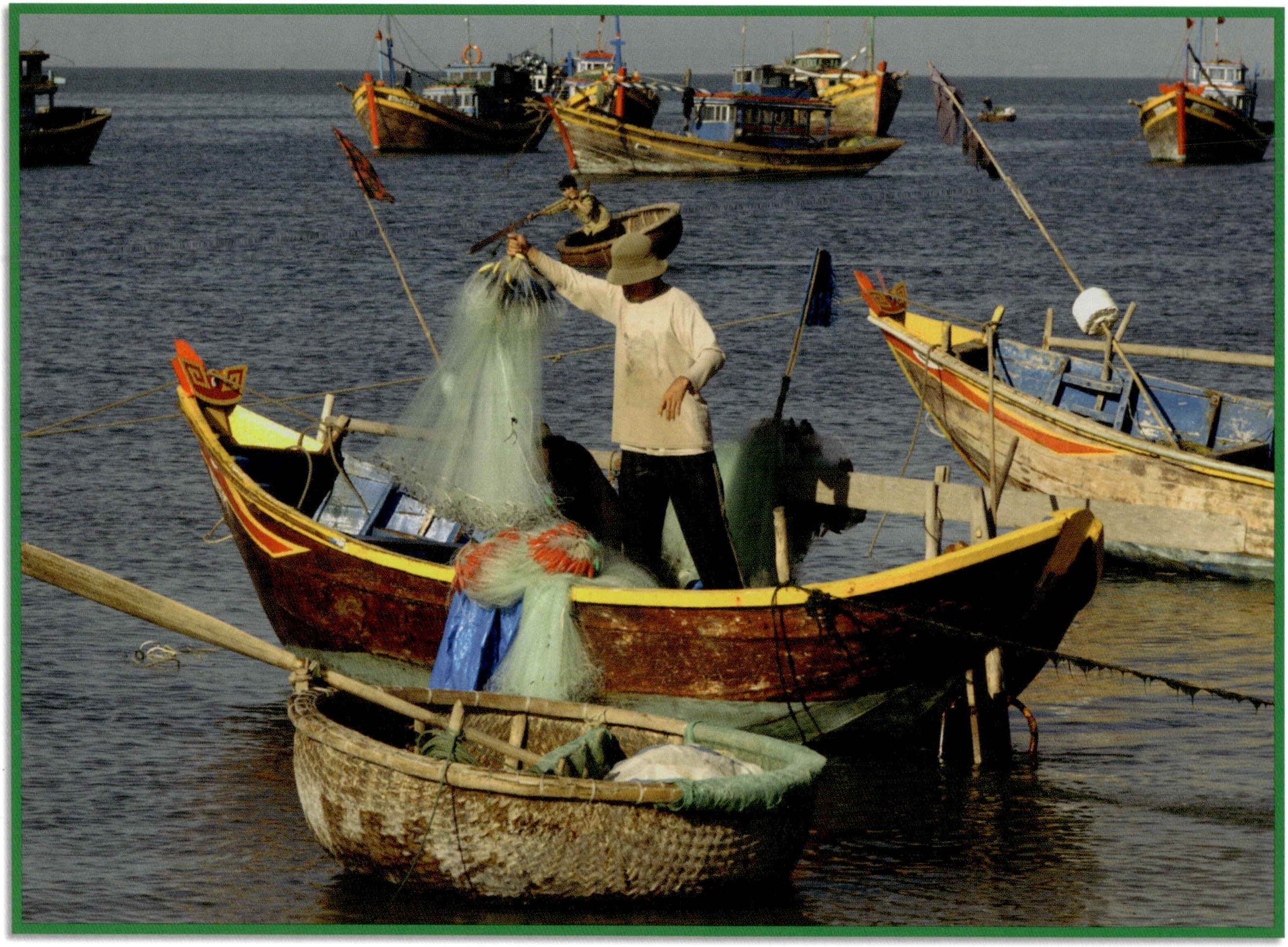

boats

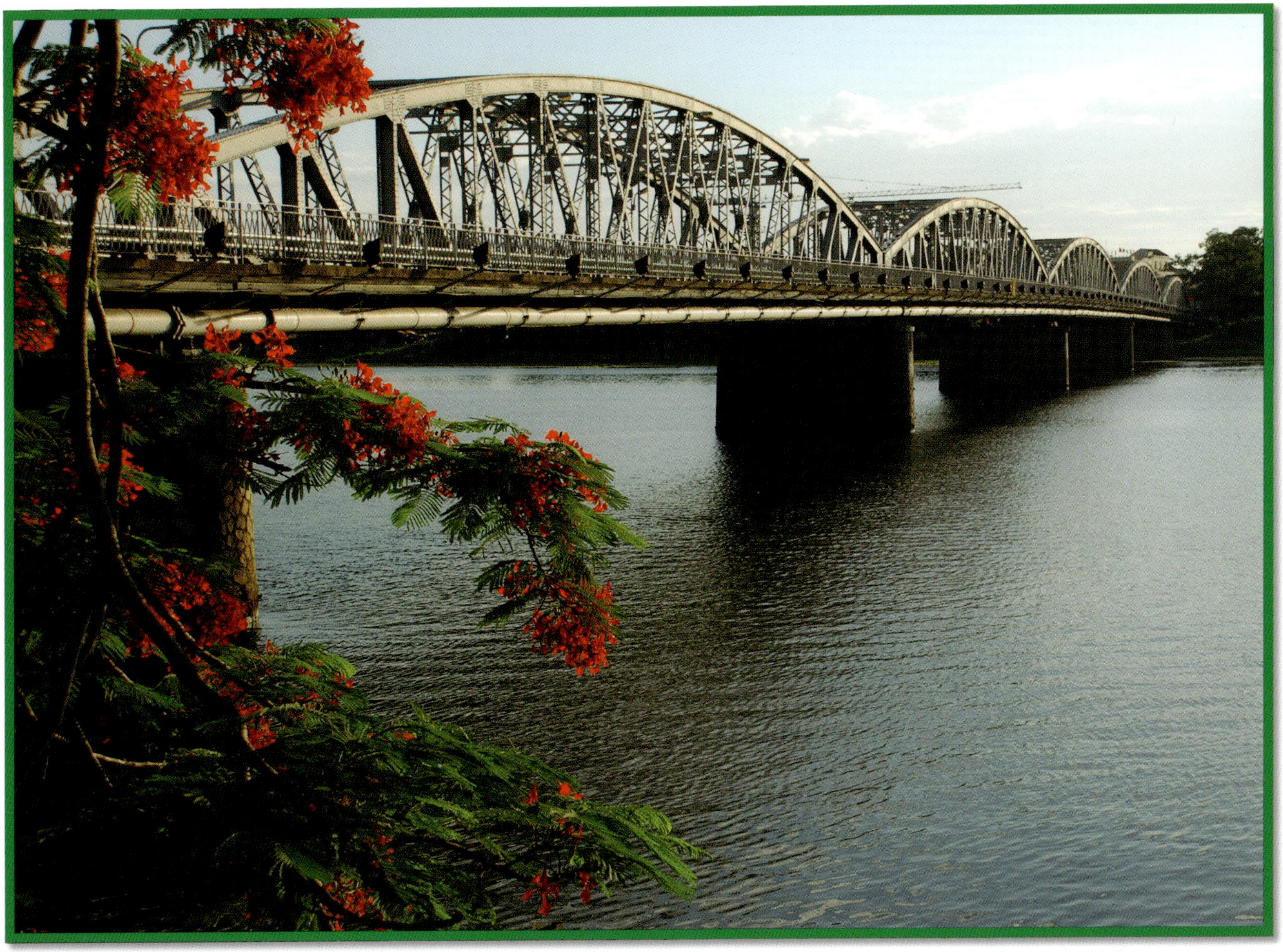

bridge

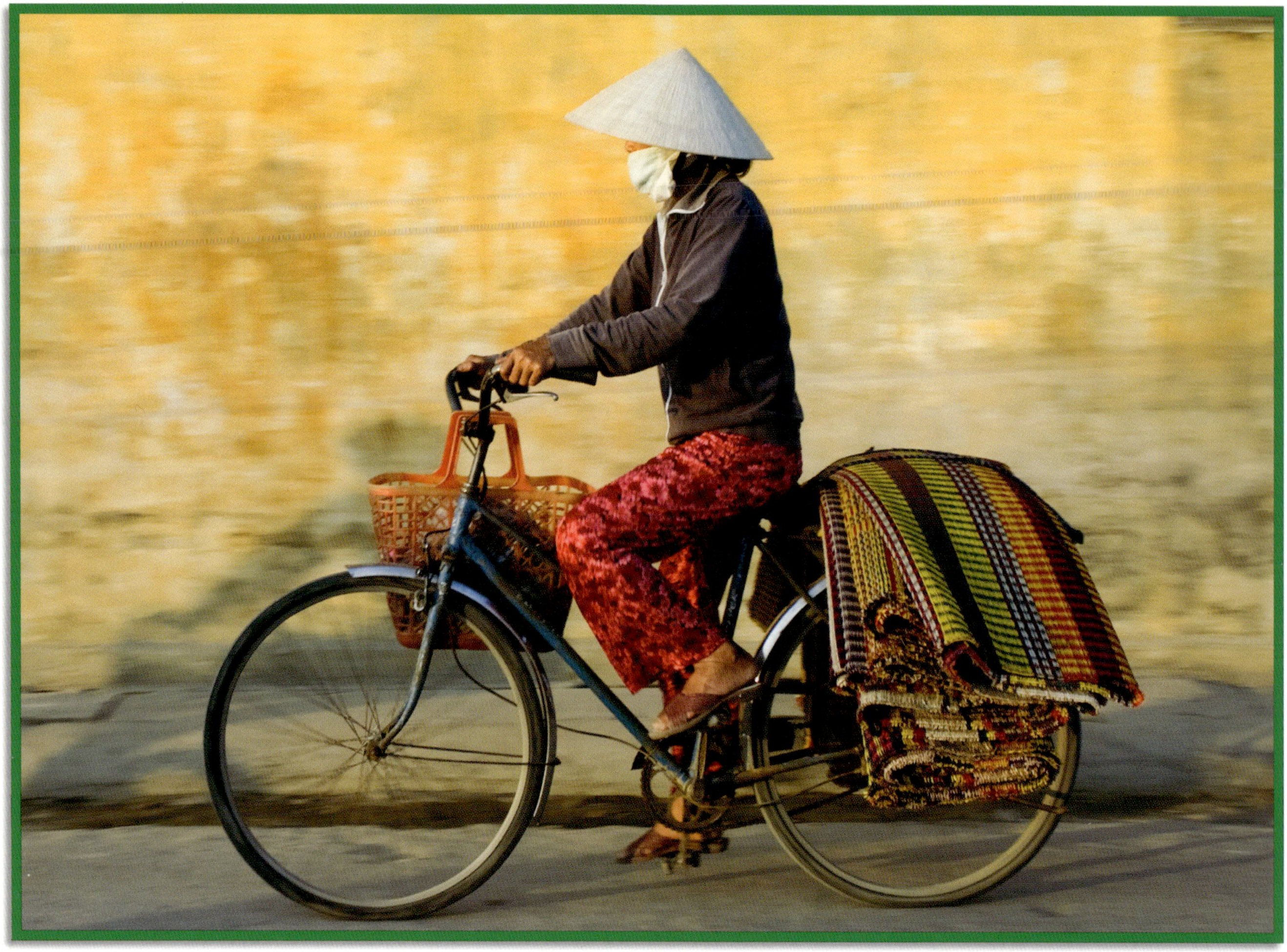

bike

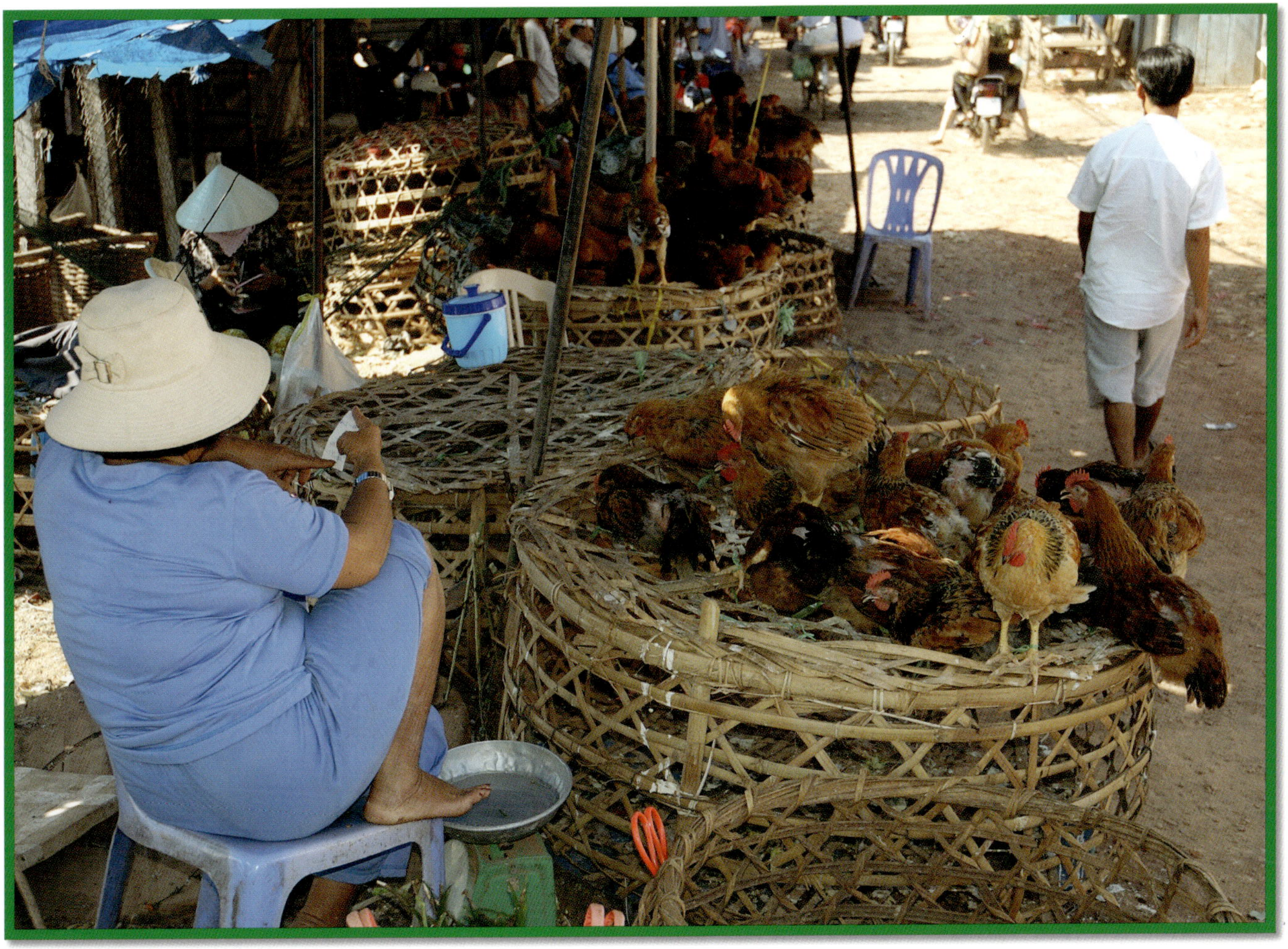

birds

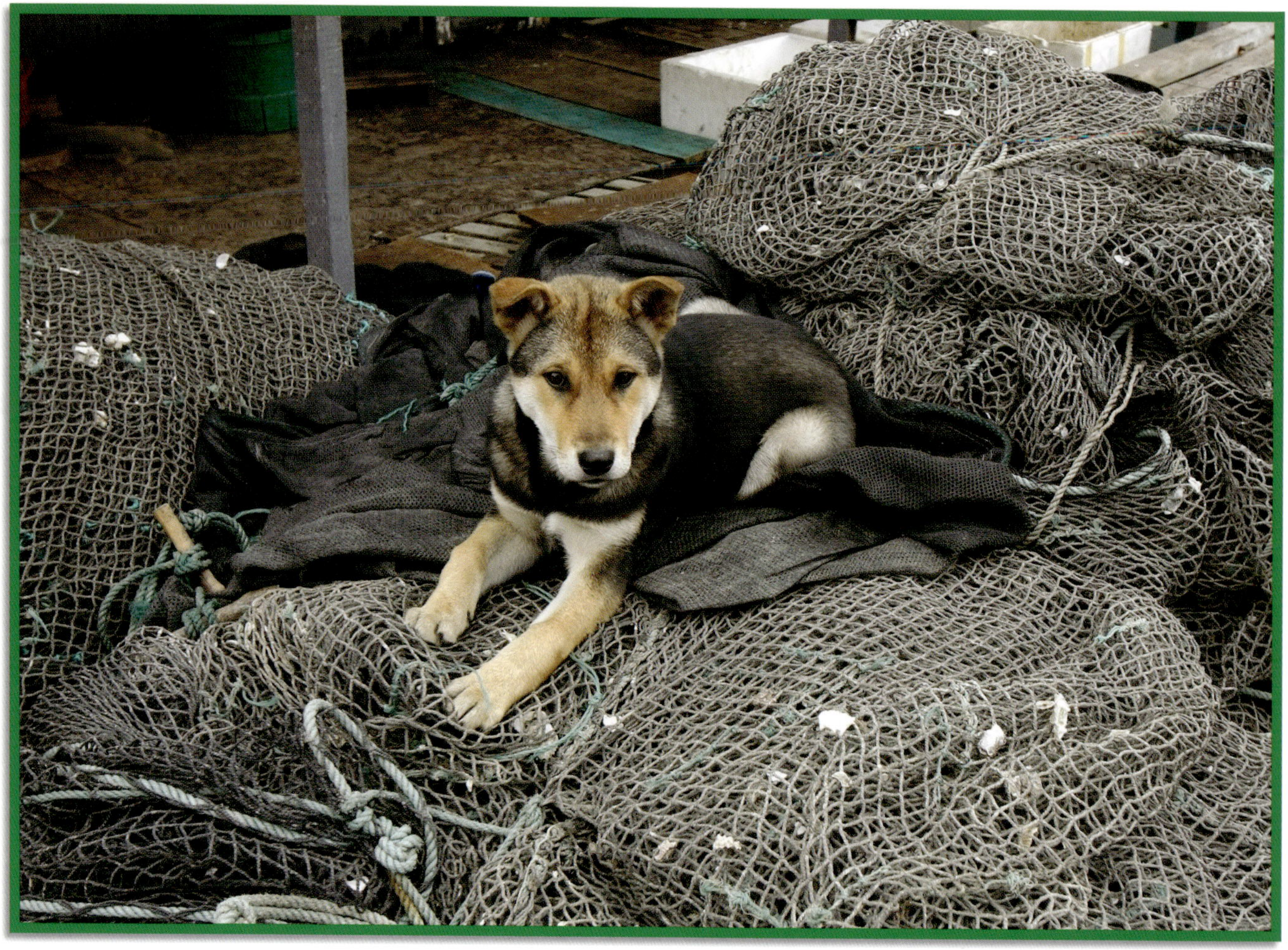

dog

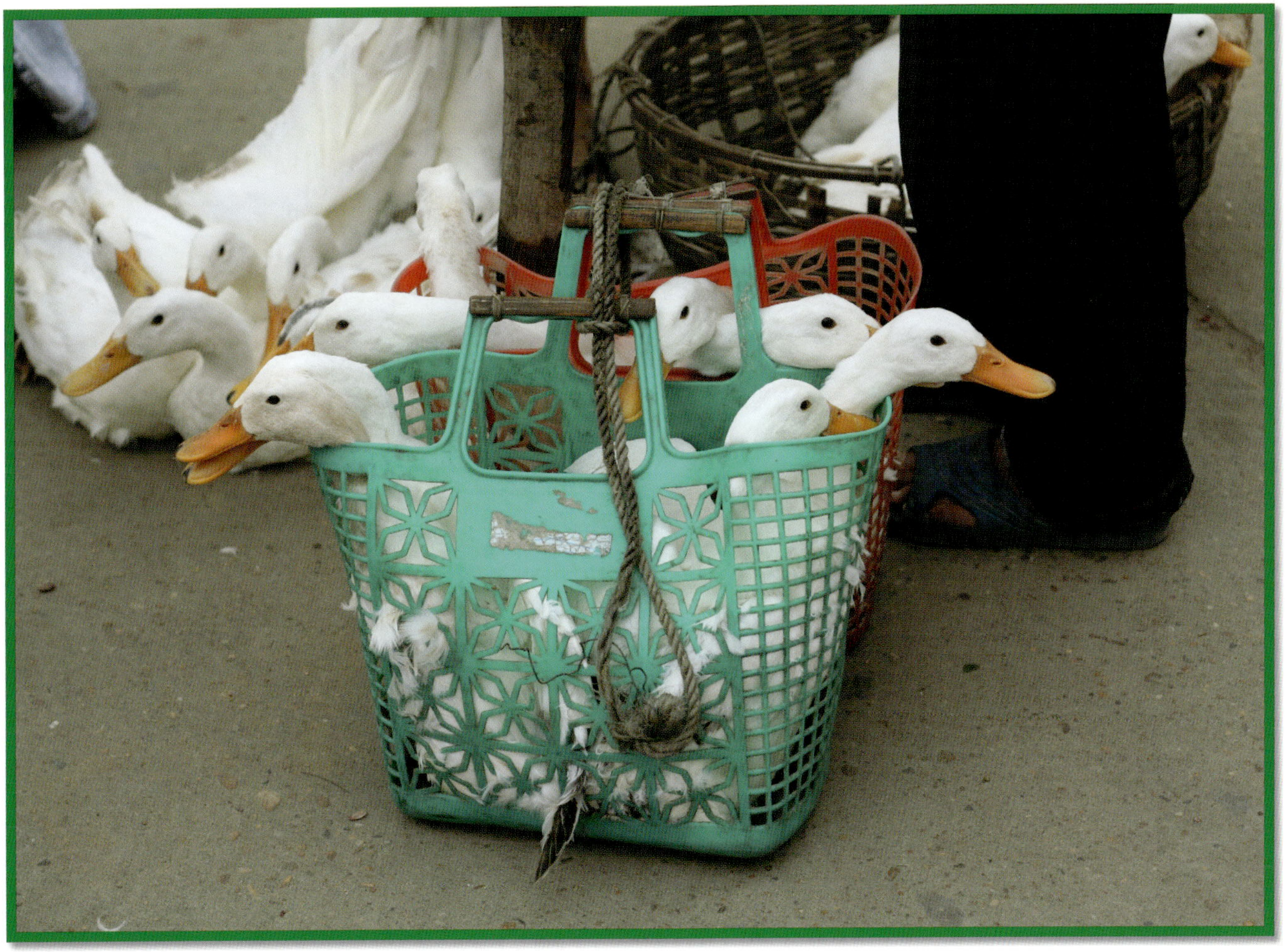

ducks

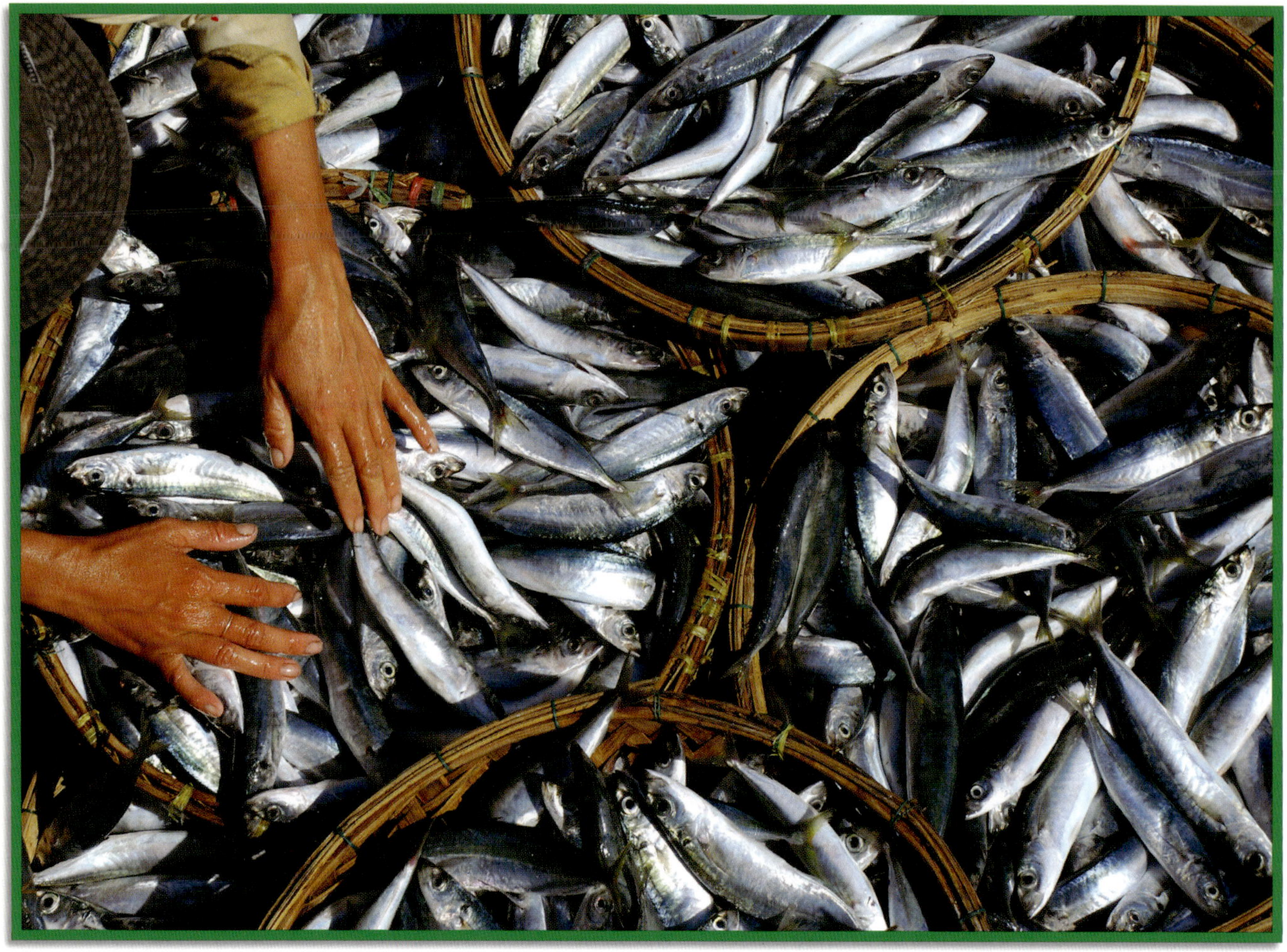

fish

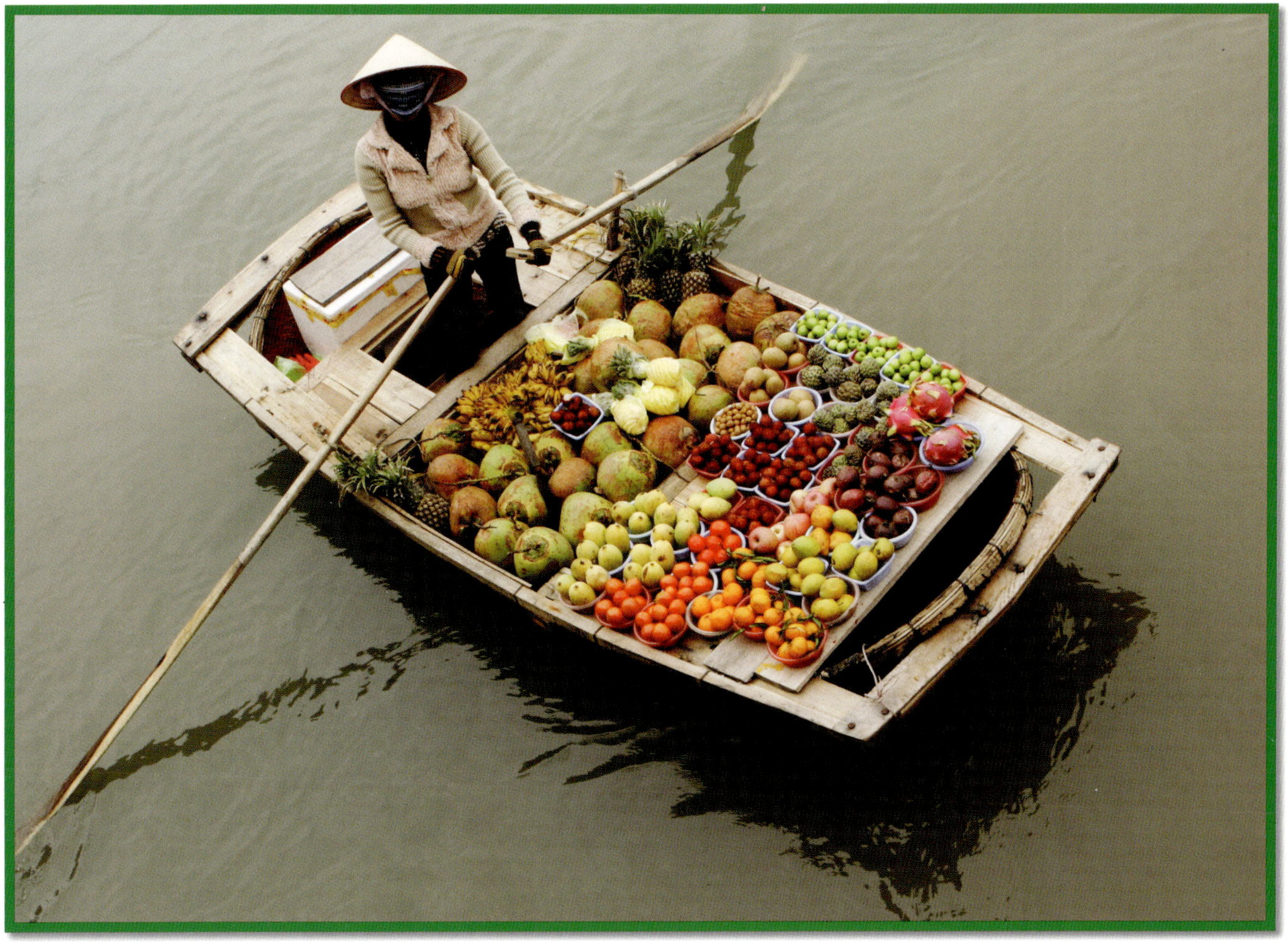

food

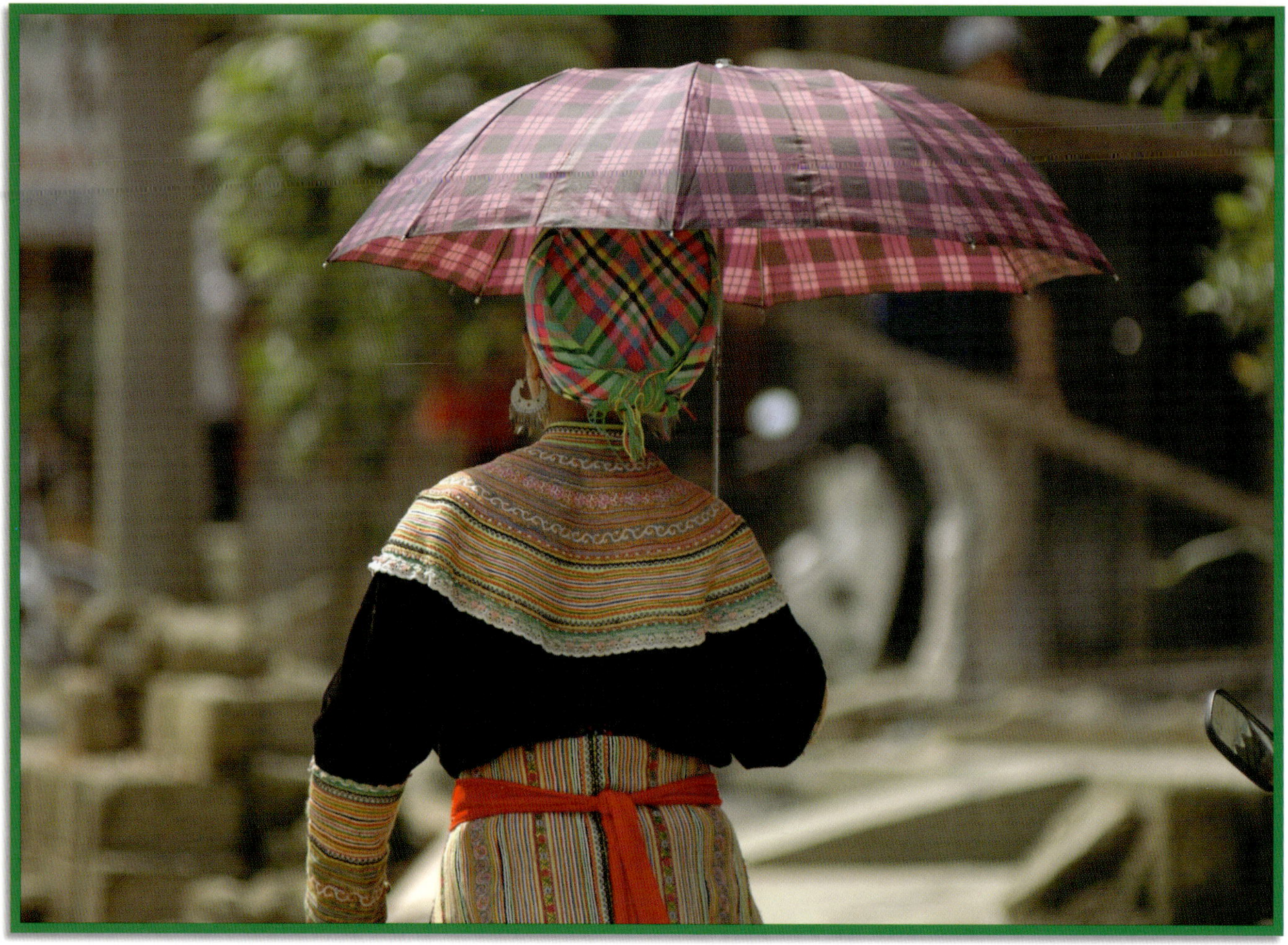

umbrella

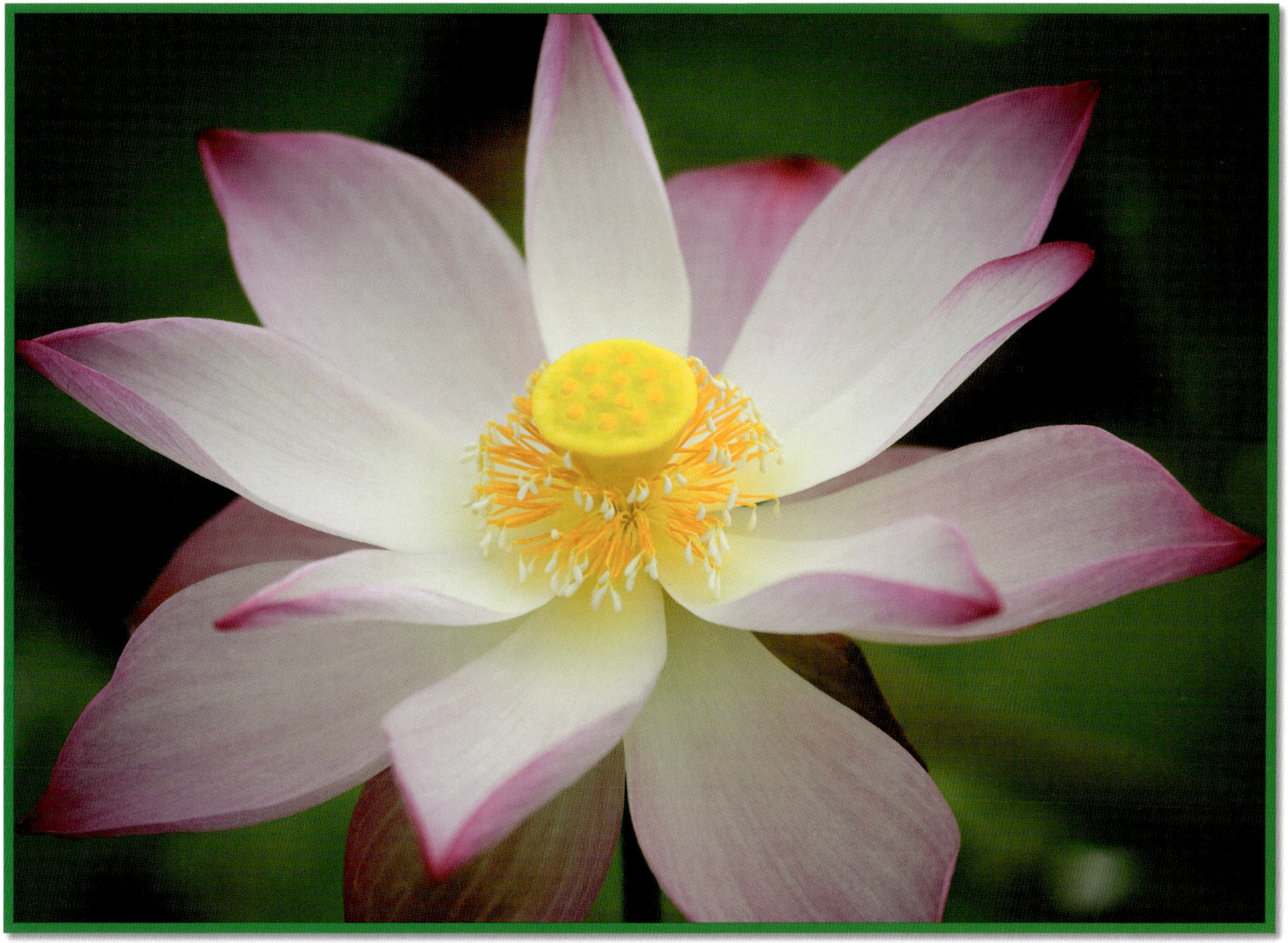

flower

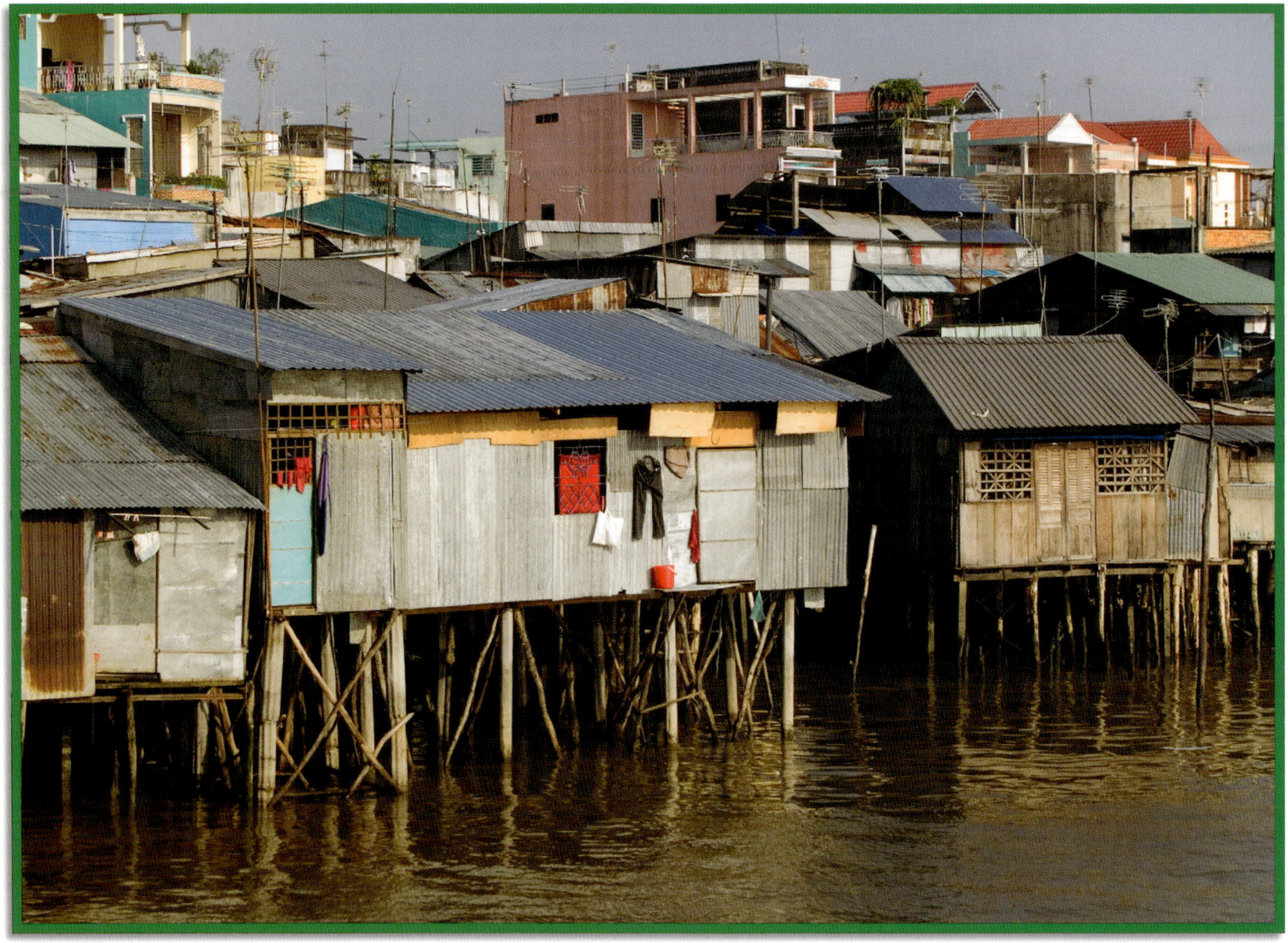

house

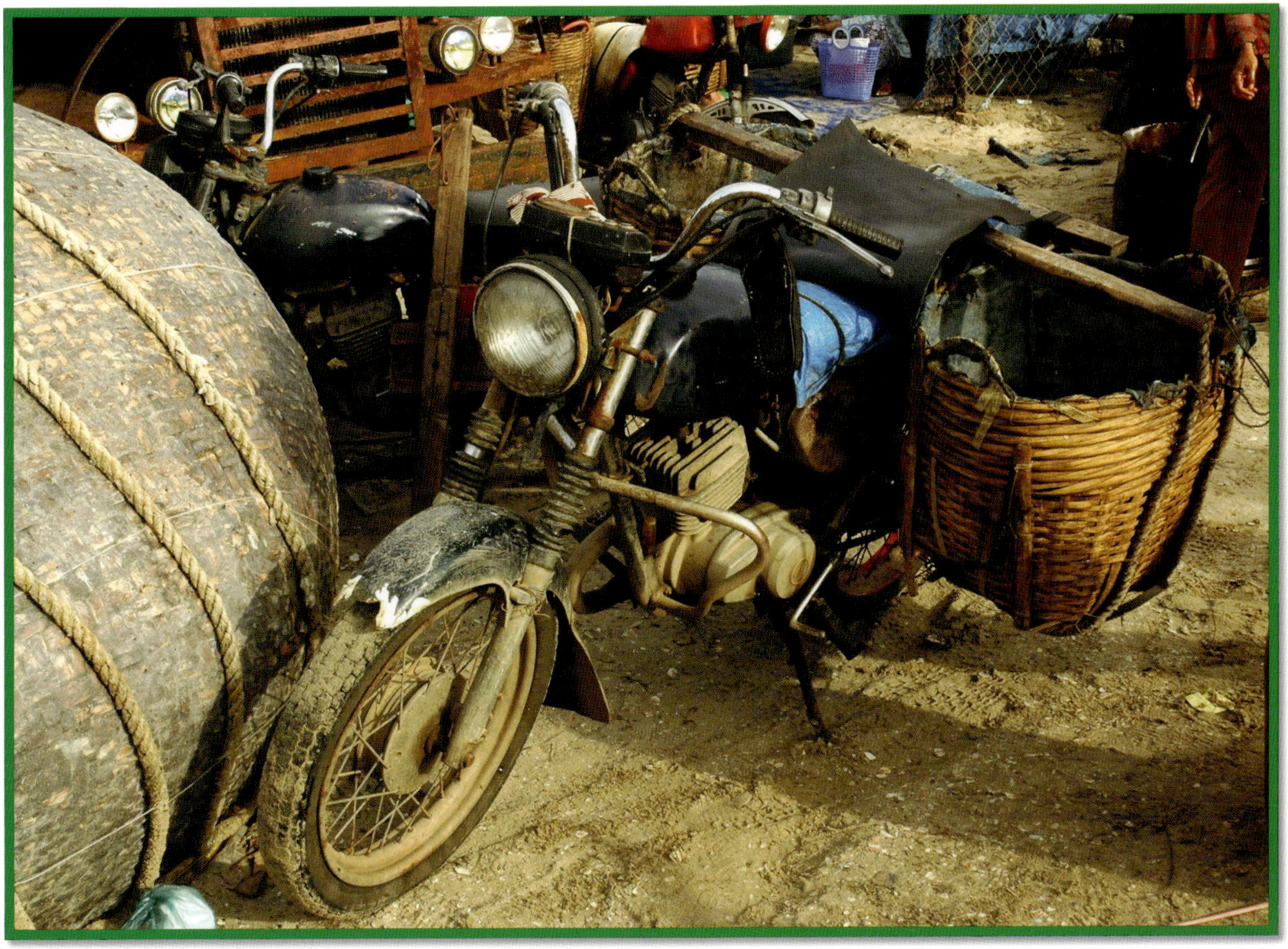

motorcycle

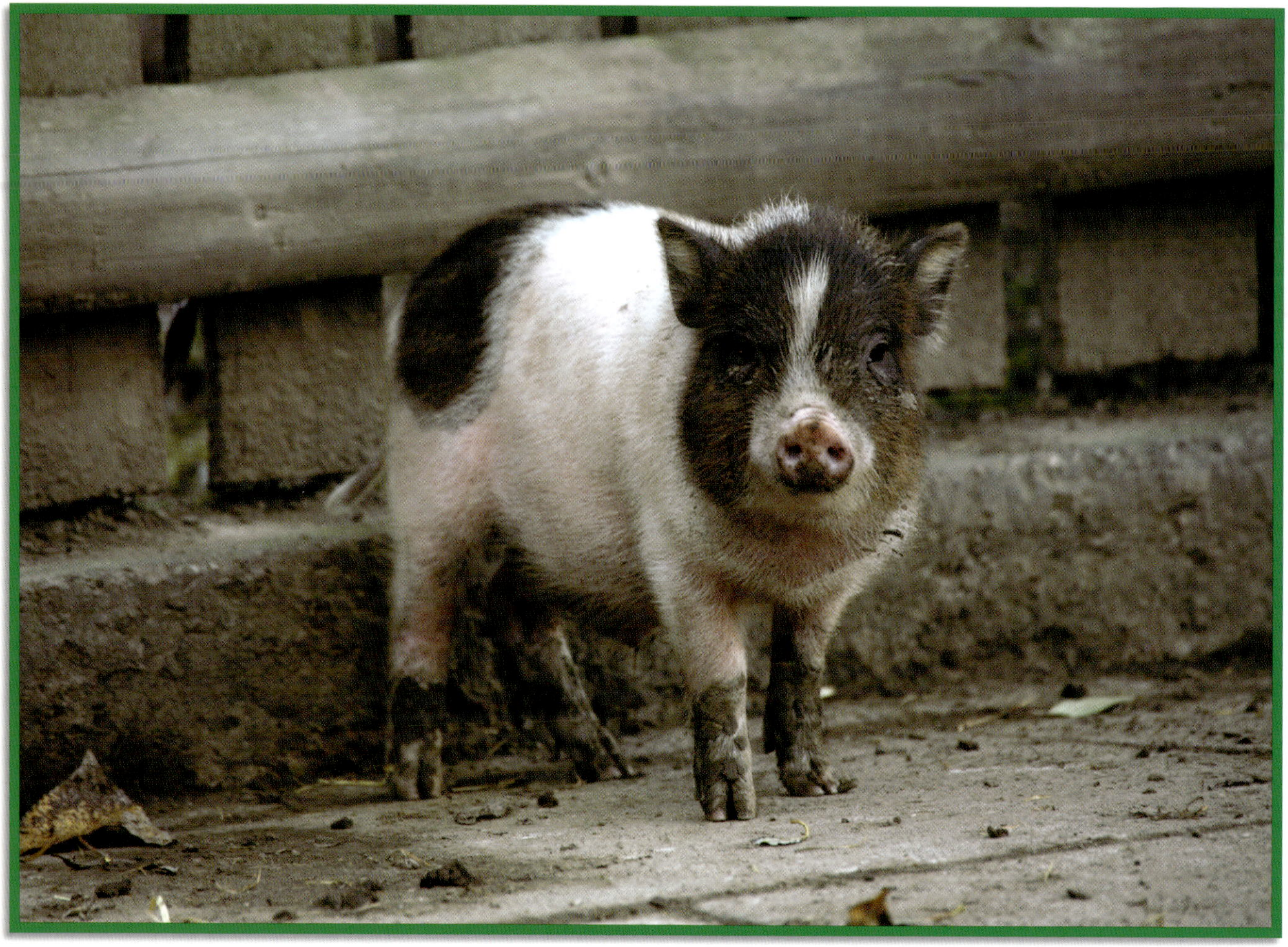

pig

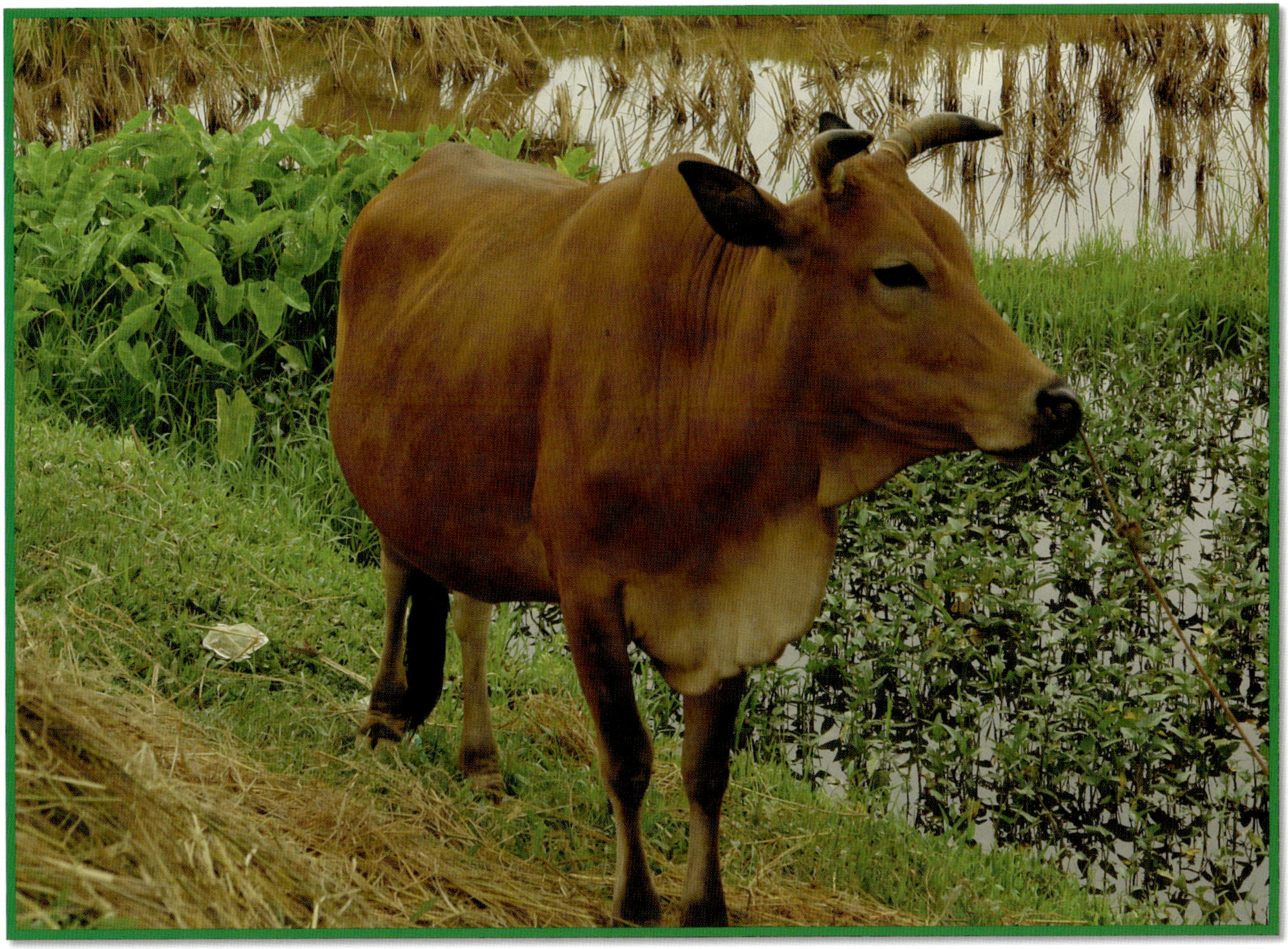

cow

Match the letter to the picture.

c

f

p

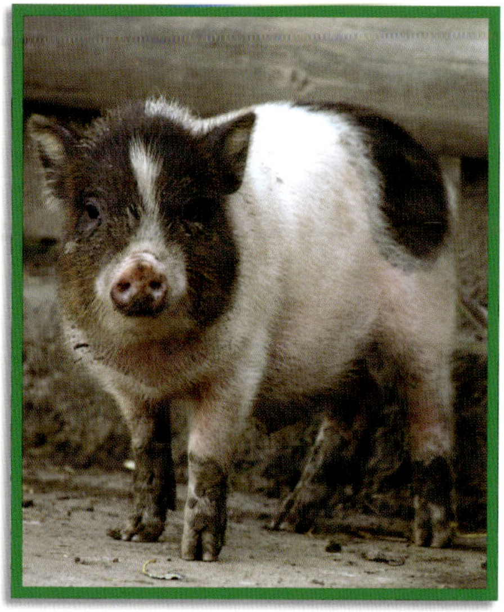

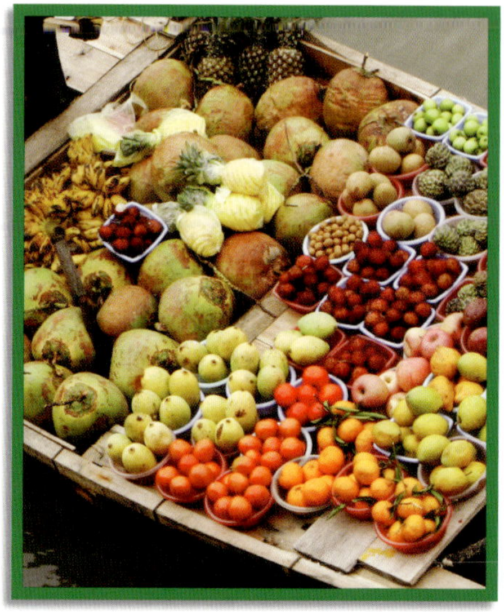

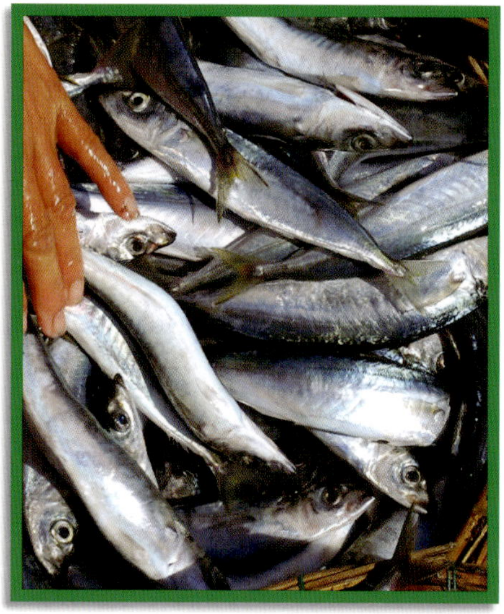

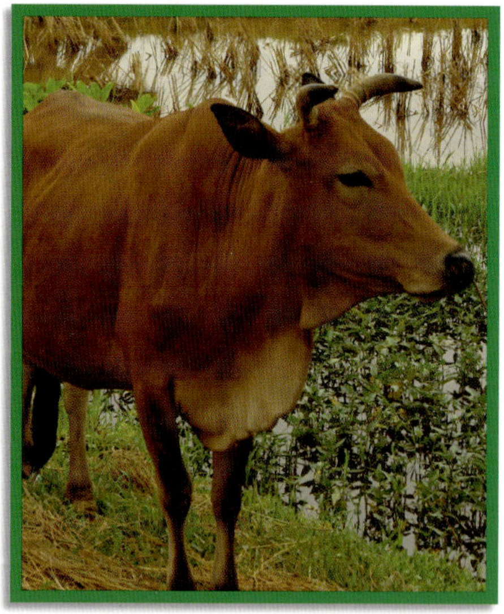